GOTCHA!

GOTCHA!

by Peter Funt & Mike Shatzkin

The Stonesong Press
a division of Grosset & Dunlap, Inc.
51 Madison Avenue
New York, N.Y. 10010

Contents

Acknowledgments

OUR THANKS . . . to some special people who helped gather material for this book and despite whose best advice we decided to have it published: Joe Dehaen, Larry Dietz, Clarence Fanto, John Moran, Barb North, Steve North and Mike Winters. Also, Paul Fargis (a publisher with a sense of humor) and the following Funts: Evelyn, Patricia, John and, of course, Allen.

Introduction

When you sneak into the room where an invalid keeps his crutches and remove the rubber tips from the bottoms, then insert a couple of half-inch wooden dowels and replace the tips so that, in effect, the crutches become longer and this fellow, in addition to all his other problems, thinks he's getting *shorter* . . . when you do that, that's not funny.

But when you sneak into the coatroom at the office where a certain loudmouthed guy you work with hangs his hat and replace the hat with an identical model a quarter-size smaller, so that this highbrow, in addition to being obnoxious, thinks his head is *swelling* . . . when you do that, *that's* funny.

A good practical joke has to be funny. It's a joke that is played on someone—a target or victim—sometimes purely for fun, sometimes out of spite. When it's played for laughs, it should seem funny to the victim as well as the joker. If it's closer to an act of revenge or retaliation, then at least it ought to elicit laughs from an impartial observer. Otherwise, it's a lousy practical joke.

I used to work at a printing company where I was the first to arrive each day at the unfunny hour of 5 A.M. As part of my routine, I always checked the boss's desk to see if there were any important messages from the night before. One morning my bloodshot eyes noticed a folded sheet of paper on the desk with the boss's name on it and the word "Confidential." Frankly, I never hesitated. I opened the note and found that the message was for me. It said, "Good morning,

1

Peter." All alone in that still-dark office I laughed out loud—no, I roared out loud for several minutes. *That* was funny.

Later in this book you will find another version of the "confidential note" gag which we call "She Snoops to Conquer." As played on me that morning, the joke was perfect, yet to this day I have no idea who was behind it. That's another thing about practical jokes: sometimes the perpetrator has to miss the payoff. No matter. If it's a good gag, the satisfaction comes from setting the trap with such care that you can imagine what happened when it was sprung.

How did the art of practical joking begin? I don't think that can be determined. In one form or another, practical jokes have probably been around as long as human nature itself.

They say Abe Lincoln was a great practical joker. More than once he is alleged to have painted a room with the help of another fellow, then, while the paint was still wet, held his partner upside down so he could make footprints in the wet paint and have it appear that someone had "walked" across the ceiling!

Old Abe, it is reported, also loved to tell a story about the way menfolk amused themselves at a hotel. When newlyweds checked in, a string was tied to the mattress in the bridal suite. The string extended through a hole in the floor down to the lobby, where it dangled from the ceiling with a bell attached. As Abe told it, the men sat in the lobby most of the night and rolled over laughing every time the bell rang. Honest.

Unfortunately, practical joking is no longer as popular as it was in Lincoln's day. Perhaps a simpler society was amused by simpler things, which is to say the hand-held joy-buzzer doesn't deliver the laughs it once did. But there is more to it than that. Nowadays, I fear, people have lost some of what it takes to laugh at life and to appreciate a good gag, even at their own expense. The modern term for this condition is—uptight. Anyone foolish enough to give a stranger a hot-foot in this day and age probably runs the risk of getting shot.

Comedian David Brenner once told a national television audience about his "favorite practical joke." The idea was to go to the service desk in a busy bank where deposit and withdrawal slips are kept and on the back of one slip write, "This is a stickup. Hand over all your cash." The slip was then returned to the stack for use by an unsuspecting bank patron.

Brenner said that as a kid he loved to stand around and wait for the laughs. But laughs were hard to find when one of Brenner's fans tried the stunt at a bank in Florida. "PRANKSTER CASHES IN ON BANK JOKE" was the headline in the *Sarasota Herald Tribune*. The story explained that an elderly man had had the misfortune to use the rigged slip and soon found himself surrounded by police. After some tense exchanges, police and bank officials wrote the whole thing off as a sick joke.

In fairness to David Brenner, he did warn TV viewers about the risks connected with the gag. And while it is hard to imagine that particular stunt ever being advisable, it may be that in a different time—Brenner's youth, perhaps—many actually did laugh at the bank bit. Certainly in what can be termed the Golden Age of Practical Joking—1920 to 1950—the prevailing view was, anything goes.

One of the most influential characters of the period was Hugh Troy, a man who could not tolerate the status quo. Many of the gags outlined in this book can be traced to Troy's remarkable imagination, which was matched only by his gall.

Troy once came upon a crew of workers digging up a street in mid-Manhattan and without skipping a beat hit on the idea of posing as their superior "from the main office." He proceeded to order the men to pick up their tools and move one block away, where they spent the rest of the afternoon digging one of the largest and least necessary holes on record.

3

While in the army Troy took an interest in the pieces of flypaper that hung from the mess hall ceiling. He devised a full-page printed report in typical military style that listed every piece by number and offered statistics on exactly how many flies were caught during each twenty-four-hour period covered by the report. For weeks he mailed the reports to Washington. Sure enough, Troy's fellow officers finally got the call: Where the hell were their Daily Flypaper Reports?

Like many true practical jokers, Hugh Troy did not always target his gags at a particular person; many were broadsides at society. Once he searched for and found a store that sold benches exactly like those in New York's Central Park. He eagerly carried his bench to the park and sat reading a paper until a policeman came along. At that point, Troy got up, took his bench and walked away, hoping the cop would try to stop him. He did. Then, with proper indignation, Troy pulled out the receipt proving to the officer that this was indeed his own *private* bench.

There is, no doubt, a little of Hugh Troy in most of us—if not his nerve, certainly his desire to at times fight back, scream out, poke fun and cause trouble. If there's a spark of such stuff in a person, it is most likely to surface when he sets foot on a college campus. Campus life, like military life, seems to bring out the best—and often the worst—in a practical joker. In such an environment things can quickly get out of hand.

One of my many college pranks was carried out in the middle of the night with the help of another fellow who even at this late date probably wishes to remain anonymous. We decided to call a local radio station in Denver with an "on-scene news report" about a nonexistent fire at a nearby women's school. The report made very little mention of the fictitious fire but provided great detail about "hundreds of coeds, forced to flee naked into the streets." The whole thing was so silly that we were just as surprised as the fire department when the report was broadcast. Still,

4

we called back several times with "updated reports," and as each hit the air, things got further out of control. The story was picked up and carried on the United Press International wires in Colorado . . . other stations saw the wire story and aired their own reports . . . crowds gathered outside the school that was supposed to be burning, apparently for a look at the nude girls . . . and finally, police had to break down the door of the radio station (which was locked tight during the night) to tell the all-night newsman to stop reading the story.

Like David Brenner's fan in Florida, we laughed for a while. But we, too, had some tense monents after reading in *The Denver Post* that the FBI was checking tapes of the broadcast in an attempt to catch those responsible for the hoax.

Actually, phony news stories are a common form of practical joke in the nation's newsrooms, but such pranks are usually for the private enjoyment of the staff and are not supposed to go out over the air or wind up in print. We know of a vice president at **ABC** News who gleefully told of calling a major New York radio station years ago and convincing the news director he was talking to Charles de Gaulle. The "interview" went on for several minutes before the caller put in a not-too-subtle plug for another station and hung up.

Even as no-nonsense an organization as *The New York Times* is not immune to the efforts of the practical joker. Back in 1966 the *Times* carried a complete list of students who had won awards at graduation from City College. Far down the list readers found the "Brett Award to the student who has worked hardest under a great handicap—Jake Barnes."

Of course there was no such award. The listing was inspired by two characters in Ernest Hemingway's *The Sun Also Rises:* Lady Brett Ashley and the sexually impotent man who loved her, Jake Barnes! The prankster turned out to be a young *Times* reporter, Clyde Haberman, who admit-

5

ted having written the entry as a gag but never intended for it to go into the paper. Haberman was banished from the staff of the *Times* but years later was allowed to return.

Almost every profession has its own form of practical joke. Usually the target is the greenhorn or newcomer to the group: Baseball players often tell about sending a rookie for a bat stretcher or other nonexistent piece of gear. New arrivals at military camp are sent looking for the rubber flag on a rainy day. An auto mechanic gets a laugh by plugging his partner's oil can with putty. The radio announcer is halfway through reading a news bulletin when someone lights the bottom of the paper with a match. A new lab worker in a hospital might spend hours puzzling over a urine sample before "analyzing" the fact that he's been given a bottle of tea.

People in show business are known to be frequent practical jokers. One trade prank is to send a telegram to a hopeful actor with the message: "Disregard my previous wire," and sign the name of a well-known producer. Comedian Tim Conway tells of appearing on *The Carol Burnett Show* and being wired, Peter Pan–style, for a "flying scene." During rehearsals the stagehands would hoist Tim about ten feet in the air, then break for lunch and leave him hanging.

Tim's tale is illustrative of the moments in life that quite accidentally lend themselves to practical joking—moments when no elaborate scheme is necessary, just someone with a sense of humor to step in and take advantage. But sometimes waiting for life's funnier moments is a damn bore. That's why we wrote this guide to practical joking—to nudge people who want to get a laugh or get even.

We have not bothered with stunts that require much money, time or effort to accomplish. Our aim is to provide a sampling of tried-and-true jokes, none of which is too harsh or cruel, and all of which, we trust, are funny. Remember, though, that funny is a funny word; it means "laughable, especially from oddness or absurdity." But Webster doesn't mention that while one person may laugh good-naturedly at your joke, another may turn around and slash your tires.

No sooner had we gathered gags for this book than those who read them began arguing about whether certain bits were funny. You, no doubt, will have mixed feelings about a few stunts and therefore should think carefully about your "victim's" outlook before pulling his leg. We wish to state for the record that in no instance are we advocating anything illegal, immoral, mean, harmful or fattening. (And if you are caught, the Secretary will disavow any knowledge of your actions.)

For this project I worked in cahoots with Mike Shatzkin, a friend even before the day we placed a piece of *Whoops!* (rubber stuff that looks remarkably like vomit) on the floor in Miss Frodsham's seventh-grade class. To let you know where we're coming from, we still think *that* was funny even if Miss Frodsham never did.

A final word of caution before you tackle the jokes that follow! Read them, relate them to your own situation, then proceed at your own risk. Remember, with this book you get a lesson, not a license.

—Peter Funt

Hard-Boiled Comedy

Okay, let's get cracking. Here's a joke you are liable to enjoy reading about but never dream of doing. Believe us, it's not as difficult as it seems and the payoff is loaded with laughs.

Your mission (should you decide to accept it) is to fill some eggs with Jell-O. Sounds simple, right? Actually it is. You begin by blowing out the eggs, a fairly common procedure when making Easter or Christmas ornaments. To do it, poke a small hole in one end of the egg and a slightly larger one in the other end. By blowing into the small hole you can empty the entire contents of the egg out the large hole. When this is done, the next step is to close the small hole with any strong glue.

Now, instead of decorating the egg—or eggs, if you are making several—mix a batch of lemon Jell-O and pour it into the hole you still have in one end of the egg. (The easiest way to do it is with a tiny funnel, although an ordinary soda straw with the top end spread open will do the job.) Fill the eggs almost to the top, then put them back into the egg carton where they will stand upright. The carton goes into the refrigerator for at least four hours so the Jell-O will harden.

When you remove the eggs, the only thing left to be done is to glue the top hole closed (use fragments of shell from another egg if you must). There you have it: the Jell-O Egg.

By now you must be wondering, what exactly is so funny about a Jell-O Egg? Well, it has many uses, all of which are hilarious. The simplest thing to do with Jell-O Eggs is to

mix a few of them in with ordinary eggs in the refrigerator so that whoever does the cooking in your house mistakes them for the real thing. When that person cracks one of these eggs he won't know what it is . . . a hard-boiled egg? a rotten egg from the store? a strange mutation? It is, for lack of a better word, freaky.

Another use for Jell-O Eggs is to pack them in a lunch, yours or somebody else's, where it will be assumed they are hard boiled. Naturally they peel just like hard-boiled eggs, but again the question: What the hell are they? This is a fine opportunity for you to express mock surprise, then boldly take a big mouthful and exclaim, "They're really not bad!"

Although we've never tried this extra touch, it was suggested that perhaps a few feathers (like those commonly found in pillows) be slipped into the egg along with the Jell-O. This tends to give Jell-O Eggs an embryogenic quality. But then, with Jell-O Eggs, there's simply no accounting for taste.

How to Drive
Them Crazy

If driving somebody crazy appeals to you, anyone with a car is sure to be rattled by this simple bit—whether or not the car he drives is a rattletrap.

Imagine the frustration of starting a car, pulling away from the curb, and immediately hearing a strange rattling sound coming from the rear. When the car stops, the noise stops, yet it starts again evey time the car is driven. An inspection of the car reveals nothing.

All it takes to accomplish this insanity is a handful of nuts and bolts and the time necessary to plant them inside the victim's hubcap. The job is done easily at night if you have access to the car when it is parked, but you can set up the gag practically anytime since it takes only a minute or two.

You might consider pulling this trick on someone who works at your office by fixing the hubcap while his car is parked during the day. Or, try this: Rig the hubcap of the guy who gives you a ride to work so you will be on hand when he discovers his strange problem. Then, while he is worrying about it at the office, switch the nuts and bolts from one rear hubcap to the other. During the ride home he's likely to stop worrying about having his car checked and start thinking about getting his ears examined.

If you have the time and inclination, we have devised an even more baffling cold-weather version of the trick. To do it, you must remove the victim's hubcap and take it home for several hours of preparation. Use the upside down hubcap as a *mold* into which you pour water (fill it a little more

13

than halfway), then drop in the nuts and bolts. Place the hubcap in a freezer until the water becomes solid ice.

Now return to the car and replace the hubcap. During the colder months of the year the ice will remain solid until the victim drives his car, at which point the nuts and bolts will gradually be released as the ice melts. This technique allows the driver to travel for several miles before he hears anything, then the rattling noise begins and slowly builds—as if the car is falling apart bit by bit.

Under Cover Assignment

Everyone knows you can't tell a book by its cover, but what about magazines?

Here's the prescription for dealing with a doctor or dentist who keeps you waiting endlessly for scheduled "appointments" or whose bills seem to rise faster than your blood pressure.

Purchase a few copies of *Time* and *Newsweek* plus a few popular women's magazines—stuff ordinarily found in waiting rooms—along with copies of *Hustler, Penthouse* and other graphic magazines not common to most doctors' offices. Be sure they are the same size and are stapled, not glued.

After reading the *Hustler* and *Penthouse*, you're ready to go to work by opening all the magazines to the center page and spreading apart the staples so they can be removed without ripping the paper. The plan is to put the innocent covers on the nasty pages.

Most of the men's magazines are about one quarter-inch larger than the news weeklies but the excess can easily be trimmed. Also, the men's magazines are so thick that some of the bland outer pages should be discarded to make your finished product about the same size as the magazine whose cover it will bear. Now put your "new" magazines together by reinserting the staples.

Next time you visit the doctor's office, simply deposit the magazines in the waiting room. You might then take a seat and watch the patients' faces light up—or blanch—as they

thumb through each magazine. The best time to work the gag is mid-morning or mid-afternoon when the office is likely to be filled with little old ladies and housewives.

We've only tried this gag once but were surprised to find that on our next visit to the doc's office—a full three weeks later—our magazines were still there. They were on the coffee table—showing signs of considerable wear!

Direct from Battle Creek

Gone are the days when the little elves at cereal companies around the country stuffed surprises of real value in your box of corn flakes. Today's consumers of cold cereal just don't know the joy of opening a box of Munchy Crunchies and finding a decoder ring, a range-finder or other valuable gift. There is nothing you can do to change the economics of the cereal business, but you can go to work on a project that will produce a surprise for the cereal fan in your family.

A close inspection of cereal packages reveals that they are sealed in such a way that someone can break in, then reseal the package so it looks as good as new. Next time there is a new box of Super Flakes in your kitchen, try pulling open the top—which is only glued shut—without ripping the outer flap. (It doesn't matter if the inner part tears because it will be covered when you reglue the top section.) Inside is usually a waxed bag, which is not glued but simply folded over several times. Again, getting in and out is no problem.

After dumping some of the cereal, you come to the fun part—deciding what "prize" to place inside. We prefer a subtle approach. For example, you might purchase from the dime store a strange toy that is almost as big as the cereal box itself so that the lucky person who opens the package at breakfast finds practically no cereal. Or, you could use an item that is strangely out of place in a cereal box such as a packaged brassiere. Rubber snakes, a stuffed mouse, or a few specimens from your butterfly collection are also good choices.

17

18

A different approach is to enclose a printed message in the box. How about a "Notice" from the factory indicating this is a test batch of cereal, produced with a new form of synthetic grain. Maybe a lengthy questionnaire for cereal consumers with probing queries such as, "How long are you able to keep a spoonful of Crispo Treats in your mouth before they lose their crunch?" The surprise that results from finding something unexpected in a *sealed* cereal box can even be used for more polite, romantic purposes. Imagine the reaction when your loved one opens a box of Monster Flakes on Valentine's Day and finds your card with the note: "I got up early and kissed each flake, so fill your bowl to the top. Today, and every day of the year, you're my snap, crackle and pop!"

There is no end to the fun you can have tampering with cereal packages. Just be careful to refold the inner bag and glue the top flap on the box so it looks store-fresh. And please resist any temptation to enclose a note saying, "Help, I'm being held prisoner at a factory in Battle Creek!"

... Get the Message?

The more gadgets there are in our lives, the greater the chances of something funny happening through their use. To put it another way, the more gadgets there are in our lives, the more practical jokers have to play with. Here's a harmless joke you can play on people who telephone you . . . by using a telephone-answering machine or standard tape recorder . . .

The gist of the bit is that callers hear a tape-recorded message that sounds, at first, like the typical instructions on a telephone-answering machine. But the message continues on and on and the callers soon find you are giving them instructions they can't possibly remember let alone follow.

.The idea is easier to understand after reading a sample message. Pretend you are the caller. You dial a friend's number . . . it rings twice . . . then you hear:

HI! THIS IS RALPH. I'M NOT HOME RIGHT NOW . . . BUT IF YOU WISH TO LEAVE A MESSAGE, I'LL RETURN YOUR CALL AS SOON AS I GET BACK. WAIT UNTIL YOU HEAR THE TONE, THEN LEAVE YOUR MESSAGE. (Pause)

IF YOU WISH TO LEAVE YOUR NAME IN ADDITION TO YOUR MESSAGE, PLEASE WAIT TEN SECONDS AFTER COMPLETING YOUR MESSAGE . . . AND LEAVE YOUR NAME. (Pause)

IF YOU WISH TO LEAVE YOUR NUMBER AS WELL AS YOUR MESSAGE AND NAME . . . YOU MUST WAIT FOR THE TEN-SECOND TONE, WHICH WILL BE HEARD APPROXIMATELY SEVEN SECONDS AFTER YOU LEAVE

YOUR NAME, ASSUMING YOU HAVE WAITED THE FULL TEN SECONDS AFTER GIVING YOUR MESSAGE. (Pause)

IF YOU SIMPLY WANT TO LEAVE YOUR NAME AND/OR NUMBER RATHER THAN AN ACTUAL MESSAGE . . . IGNORE THE FIRST AND SECOND TONES AND LISTEN FOR THE BUZZ. ALLOW FIVE SECONDS AFTER THE BUZZ, THEN LEAVE YOUR NAME AND/OR NUMBER. (Pause)

IF, BY CHANCE, YOUR MESSAGE AND/OR NAME AND/OR NUMBER IS INTERRUPTED BY TWO QUICK BEEPS . . . THAT MEANS YOU ARE ABOUT TO RUN OUT OF TIME ON THE TAPE. IN THAT CASE, SIMPLY REDIAL AND REPEAT THE PROCEDURE. THANKS FOR CALLING!

The idea is to confound your callers by giving them instructions that sneak up on them, then drive them crazy. To do it, you need the type of phone machine that allows an announcement of unlimited length. With that type of machine, you're all set to go.

If you don't have a phone unit—or if yours does not allow a long announcement—the gag can be worked with a standard tape recorder. First, record your announcement (no laughing) on tape and end it with something that sounds like a tone—the noise of your alarm clock will do. Cue the tape to the beginning of your spiel so it is ready when the phone rings. The easiest method of playback is to hold the phone close to the speaker (keep the playback volume very low and press the mouthpiece of the phone up against the speaker).

A much better playback system involves the use of "phone clips," which are available for a few dollars at any audio supply shop. These come with instructions showing you how to unscrew the mouthpiece of your phone and clip the two wires leading from the recorder to the terminals inside the phone. This produces a crisp, clear sound and makes it impossible for the caller to tell that an actual phone machine is not being used. Phone clips also allow you to hold the receiver to your ear so you can listen to the remarks of the caller.

Whichever method you use for playback of the tape, your

recorder must be on and ready to be started after only two or three rings of the phone. If you have doubts about the strength of the gag, go back and reread the sample announcement. Do it out loud with a no-nonsense, business-like approach. See if you can get through it without laughing.

When we tried this bit, not only did it confuse the hell out of callers—it kept working even after we confessed the trick. One friend, after falling twice for the same recording, said, "I'm never calling you again unless you disconnect that damn phone machine, or at least get a more modern one with instructions that normal people can understand!"

Hearing
Is Believing

As chillingly proved by Orson Welles on Halloween eve, 1938, radio is perhaps the most powerful medium for perpetrating a hoax. It was Welles, of course, who played the starring role in "War of the Worlds"—the CBS Radio drama about an invasion from Mars that caused widespread panic among thousands of listeners.

Although the broadcast began with a straightforward announcement that what was to follow was mere fiction, there were many believers when a news reporter began telling about a cylinder of unknown origin landing "with almost earthquake force" near Grover's Mill, New Jersey. More details were soon added about serpentlike beings "with saliva dripping from rimless lips that seem to quiver and pulsate." Then, the terrible news: "Ladies and gentlemen, as incredible as it may seem, both the observations of science and the evidence of our eyes lead to the inescapable assumption that those strange beings who landed in the Jersey farmlands tonight are the vanguard of an invading army from the planet Mars!"

That did it. Additional reports of panic, destruction and the declaration of martial law were just icing on the cake. But the broadcasters never dreamed that outside their studio, in the real world, actual panic was occurring as hospitals treated victims of shock, police were swamped with calls and a power shortage in a small Midwestern town at the height of the drama sent thousands of people into the streets screaming for help. When the broadcast ended,

24

25

Welles and the network had a lot of explaining to do for police and reporters, who had already gathered outside the studio. But ultimately, "War of the Worlds" proved to be the best thing that could have happened for the career of Orson Welles.

Do not plan on advancing your own career by tampering with the output of your radio, but do consider the fact that hearing is believing—especially when what is heard comes from an "official" broadcast source.

There are several ways to fool people with a phony radio broadcast; none that we know of is simple, but all are quite workable. One scheme involves wiring the output of an amplifier or tape recorder to the speaker of an ordinary radio. This is best done with a table model radio that allows easy access to the components by simply removing the back of the set. Once that is done, you merely attach your lead wires to the speaker itself so that whatever you "broadcast" from the next room will be heard from the radio speaker. An even easier setup is to work with a stereo system that uses speakers that are not attached but rather sit elsewhere in the room. You can wire directly onto their terminals.

Your "broadcast" originates from a hiding place elsewhere in the house and features either your own voice or that of an accomplice by way of the microphone or previously recorded tape. We leave it to your own imagination to devise a fitting script but suggest your gag be based on something more plausible than an invasion from Mars. Usually the stunt works best with something that strikes close to home such as the announced arrival of a celebrity in that community . . . a contest that the listener has just won . . . or a warning about something. (One favorite "warning" joke is to announce that the water in the community will be shut off for several hours and that residents have only fifteen minutes in which to fill bathtubs, pots and other containers with as much water as they are likely to need.)

One fellow we know managed a very convincing radio hoax with his car radio and a cassette tape machine. As is the case in many autos, Bob's radio and tape systems played through the single set of car speakers. Therefore, all he needed for the gag was a prerecorded tape (voiced by a friend) that began with some ordinary music and continued with a strange announcement from the DJ.

With the tape ready to go, he took an unsuspecting girl for a ride. After a while, Bob suggested they listen to the radio and casually snapped it on. But he had actually disconnected the "on-off" control on the radio and attached it to the power control for the cassette machine. So while Diane thought he was turning on the radio, he was really turning on the tape, and since it began with a record—already halfway through—and was heard from the regular speakers, she was set up perfectly for the gag. When the record ended, the DJ announced that the song was "dedicated to a great couple, Bob and Diane." Naturally, Diane was surprised to hear this coming from Bob's car radio and was even more startled when the announcer said Bob's postcard had been selected at random, entitling him to dinner for two at a fancy restaurant. (That night, Bob secretly paid the tab. His real "prize" was the date he had arranged thanks to his radio hoax.)

Still another method of pulling a radio trick is to use a miniature radio transmitter that sends out your broadcast without the need to hook up wires to the victim's receiver. We found one such AM transmitter in kit form for $7.95 at a major audio store. Its range was listed as 40 feet, which is certainly good enough for use from one room to another. The one drawback with this gadget is that your signal must be broadcast on a vacant frequency—that is, at a place on the dial where there is no existing signal in your area. This means you must pretune the victim's radio and hope he or she leaves the dial set after the radio is on. Or, you can walk in while the victim is listening and casually switch to something else (the frequency you are using).

27

The salesman in the audio shop explained that he and his co-workers often used an FM transmitter to pull practical jokes on customers. The transmitter was set up in the back room of the store where the selling floor was visible through a two-way mirror. One of the salesmen would demonstrate an FM tuner to an interested buyer by turning the dial from one station to the next and finally positioning it at the vacant spot where nothing could be heard. At that point, the salesman would pretend to be called away and excuse himself for a moment. Left alone with the radio, the customer invariably reached for the dial to tune in some music. Just as his hand neared the set, a voice—broadcast from the back room—would say, "Hey! What are you doing? The salesman told me not to let anyone touch my controls until he got back."

Most customers were understandably shocked by the voice until the truth of the matter dawned on them. At that point they usually chuckled their way into such a good mood that they gladly purchased something.

Clearly, there are countless ways to use radio for pulling a stunt. But there is a macabre footnote to the "War of the Worlds" hoax that bears reporting. When a tape of the show was played on a station in South America there was some, but not much, panic among members of the radio audience. However, when the program ended and listeners were reminded that spacemen had not actually destroyed New Jersey, crowds attacked the radio station, setting fire to the building and killing several announcers.

Borrowing
Some Laughs

Here are two versions of a How to Drive a Deserving Person Nuts routine. In one, you don't borrow something but say you did; in the other, you do borrow something—but what? These gags work well in the office or at a neighbor's home or apartment to which you have access when the people are out.

1. Scribble a note that clearly says you were in a rush, clearly says you had to borrow something, clearly says you will treat it with care and clearly promises that it will be returned when you get back after the weekend. The only thing not perfectly clear is what the devil you borrowed. Your note must be scrawled so that everything else is legible, but the item you are talking about is undecipherable. In fact, you have not borrowed anything! Your friends are left to wonder and search the house—or office—trying to determine what's missing.

2. In this version, you actually borrow something and leave a polite note—but what's illegible is your name. This works best in a busy office where you might take, say, a typewriter and leave a note that could be from any one of a hundred people!

Guess Who's Coming to Dinner

The office environment provides a natural setting for practical jokes—perhaps because it is a place where frustrations often build, where petty jealousy thrives and where people are forced to spend a great deal of time with others whom they do not necessarily like.

This particular gag takes advantage of yet another frequent occurrence where numbers of people work: the office romance. The essence of the bit is that you will create a "romance" between two people in the office by actually playing both sides. You might choose as your targets a newcomer and a person who has been around for a while. In any case, resist the temptation to make the match-up too unreasonable because the success of your joke hinges on both victims' willingness to believe they see something in each other. Also, it would be wise to pick people in separate departments who do not ordinarily have contact during the day so as to delay the chances of their actually discussing the situation.

You might begin with notes to both the victims. (These can be left on their desk, sent through interoffice channels or mailed to their home.) In each of the notes you should make a proper introduction and perhaps indicate that while you tend to be shy about talking to people, especially those you have not been formally introduced to, you would like to get to know this person better. It might even be a good idea to suggest that you (that is, the person you are pretending to be) have a burned-out romance going with

someone else in the office so, for the time being, you would rather not be seen talking to someone new. Suggest that the other person write you a letter telling something about him or herself. (At this point you must adapt the gag to the particular situation at your office. If, for example, you plan to ultimately reveal your role in the joke, you can give each of the victims *your* address and let them send their letters to your home with the other person's name on the envelope. If you would rather protect your identity, then perhaps the notes can be left at a "secret" place in the building where you can pick them up.)

Now you will be receiving two letters—one from the guy who thinks a particular girl wants to learn more about him, and one from a girl who thinks a certain guy is interested in hearing about her. Digest the contents of the notes and write back in the appropriate way.

Next step: send flowers to the woman and some little gift to the man. If all is working well at this point, you may be tempted to play it along for a while, but be careful since eventually the people involved will make it their business to meet face to face and that is something you should enjoy controlling as well. Therefore, your next move is to arrange a date. Again, offer an excuse for some secrecy and suggest to each that they meet at a particular restaurant (which you have selected and called to make a reservation). Let it go at that. Who knows, they might actually fall for each other but always be puzzled by the strange way their courtship began.

Now consider this variation: You can work the joke differently by playing just one side of the romance and letting the other person play his or her self. You might, say, communicate with a new woman at the office by pretending to be one of your male co-workers. He knows nothing about it until the end when he gets a mysterious note from this woman (which you have written) inviting him to dinner. You might even arrange to have this get-together at her place. The result is that one person goes on what is basically a "blind date" with someone who thinks the two of them have been communicating for some time.

The latter routine offers endless possibilities. For instance, you can give exciting details about the life of the man you are playing, which, of course, are all wrong. Let him straighten the facts out when they meet. You can even send a picture to the woman (a photo of your cousin who lives 2,000 miles away) and then let the real guy explain the change in his appearance in real life. Or, you might tell the woman that while you can't risk talking to her at the office, it would be nice if she acknowledged your notes by giving you a "signal" when she sees you at work. Maybe she could pull her left ear and wink twice when she passes your desk. Let the guy whose name you are using try to figure out what the hell this woman's gestures mean.

If you are playing just one part in the drama, you can fake the ultimate communication by telephoning the woman and pretending to be someone else at the office. With the phone at your disposal there is no end to the relationship you can create prior to inviting the woman to dinner with the guy whom you have been impersonating.

Signs
of the Times

A simple printed sign with the words MENS ROOM can do incredible things. It was always good for laughs in the hands of the *Candid Camera* staff. It all hinged on where the sign was placed—most memorably on the door of an ordinary clothes closet in the lobby of a movie theater.

Signs of all types offer endless possibilities for the practical joker, mostly because they are so readily believed. People are conditioned to accept information on a printed sign at face value and usually heed the sign's advice without stopping to think.

BACKWARDS ZONE. Now there's an example of an outrageous sign posted by the *Candid Camera* people on a busy sidewalk. For an entire day, passersby stopped, checked the sign and turned around to walk backwards through this special "zone." When necessary, the show's staff people would silently walk through backwards to set a proper example—which is something you can do if you wish to experiment with some of the more crazy signs.

STEP ON BLACK SQUARES ONLY! Can you guess where that sign was tried? It was posted in a hallway that was covered with black and white squares of linoleum. Never fails.

BENCH FOR BUMS ONLY. This official-looking sign was attached to a park bench.

KNOCK AFTER ENTERING. Now there's a sign that leaves most people confused about whether they're coming or going.

Bathrooms, as noted, offer many possibilities. One gag involves replacing the MEN and WOMEN signs with a pair that

34

read: OURS and THEIRS. Sometimes you can fool people without even removing the signs. How about an arrow under the MENS ROOM sign that points to the LADIES ROOM and another arrow under the LADIES ROOM sign pointing back to the MENS ROOM?

Outside an elevator you might try posting a hand-lettered sign that cautions: UP ONLY.

And of course one that never fails is DRY PAINT. No one can pass that sign without touching the wall to be sure it really is dry.

While you're at it, place a small sign next to a cigar box and leave it outside on the sidewalk. The sign should read: DONATIONS PLEASE. Some people simply won't hesitate to give to a worthy cause.

Laughs
in a Bottle

When you fill your cup from one of those water coolers—the kind with the big glass bottle—and you gaze inside at the crystal-clear, refreshing liquid, the last thing you expect to see is something gazing back at you!

Here are tips on placing the fish, animal, or other foreign substance of your choice in the water cooler where you believe it will do the most good. You'll need a few minutes when you can work on the cooler without being seen. First step is to remove the large water bottle, which, on most units, can easily be lifted off. Do this by tilting the bottle sharply toward you. Some water will spill into the cooler's own reservoir as you lift the bottle to an upright position.

Now, what to dump in the bottle? A live fish seems to bring the best reactions, but a live eel is also good, as is a live water snake. Less adventurous pranksters might settle for a rubber reptile, a large selection of which is available in most toy stores or joke shops. Remember, whatever you decide to use for the gag must be narrow enough to fit through the neck of the bottle.

If you are using a live helper, stuff a small section of wire screening into the neck of the bottle. This device will prevent the fish or other creature from slipping down into the cooler's mechanism after the bottle is replaced. Finally, return the bottle to its stand, again letting some water pour into the cooler's reservoir as you tilt the bottle.

At many offices, people tend to gather around the water cooler to chat and avoid whatever they are supposed to be

doing. For this group, you might skip the live bait in favor of something more exciting—like vodka. We suggest a quart of vodka will do the trick (you can always dump some water out of the bottle to make your office cocktail more potent).

With a quart of vodka in the water cooler, there's no telling how thirsty the office staff will become. Spiking the cooler can also lead to some memorable office parties!

A Pain
in the Rain

Not all practical jokes hinge on a sophisticated scheme carried out with Mission Impossible finesse. Some, like the one described here, are just ha-ha silly. But when a gag like this works, it brings a welcome smile to the victim as well as to the trickster.

This joke should be played on someone old enough to be slightly absentminded on occasion, or young enough to be easily duped. The target of the gag must own a pair of black or brown rubbers and you must be able to gain access to the place where the rubbers are stored. You'll need some waterproof paint (pink is the best color but white or off-white will do), plus some washable black or brown paint, the kind used in kindergarten that's mostly water—and a brush.

On your first visit, paint a set of toes on the rubbers with the waterproof paint. Your work can be literal or impressionistic, depending on your talents. Wait until the paint is fully dried and return with the washable stuff. This time paint over the toes, restoring the rubbers as closely as possible to their original appearance. (Washable paint usually dries quickly so you can apply a second coat if necessary. A few dabs of shoe polish might help. And a good final touch is to sprinkle some dirt or dust on the rubbers to help disguise your work.)

Next time your victim ventures out in the rain, he won't get far before the "toes" begin to show through. Mind you, we are not suggesting that the guy will actually think he is

seeing *his* toes—he'll simply be stuck for the rest of the trip with a set of clownishly funny footware. (If, by chance, you find someone who *does* think his toes are sticking out . . . save his name and address. He's the perfect guinea pig for every gag in this book.)

The Poison Postmark

So you've been looking for a way to get back at the fellow down the block. Well, if he has a wife who tends to be suspicious, he's sure to love you for this.

If he travels on business, the best time to strike is a few days after he returns from a trip. Purchase a sweet and delicate greeting card—you know, the kind with a puppy on the front and some syrupy sentiment inside. In longhand (get a woman to do this if you can't do it right) write a mysterious message in the card, such as:

Dearest Howard,

Thank you for being so understanding. I know you are right, it's not the quantity but the quality of time people have with each other that really counts.

X X X,

Monica

Address the envelope to your former friend Howard at his home (no return address) and put a stamp on it. Now write another note on plain paper saying:

Dear Sirs:

Recently my collection of U.S. postmarks was destroyed by a fire at our home. I am trying to start over and would appreciate your dropping the enclosed envelope in the mail.

Thank you.

This note, plus the sealed card for Howard, goes in yet another envelope addressed to "Postmaster" in the city that Howard has just visited. The card will arrive in the mail back at Howard's home bearing the postmark of the city, and you can bet his wife will take it from there.

(If you want to add a special touch, put a few drops of cheap perfume on the back flap of the envelope before sending it to the out-of-town post office. This will allow Howard's wife to pick up the scent so she can begin tracking down the guilty party.)

Warning: Don't expect to wait a few days and then reveal your joke at Howard's house. Howard might believe it was you, but his wife won't. She probably will accuse Howard of sending you over to "confess" just to get him off the hook.

There are, of course, many ways to plant the seeds of suspicion without going through the mails. Perhaps you will find inspiration in a Henny Youngman classic (circa 1950) in which two men are changing clothes at their golf club and one says to the other, "Hey Bob, how long have you been wearing that girdle?" To which Bob replies, "Ever since my wife found it in the glove compartment of my car!"

You get the idea.

43

Dressed
to Kill (You!)

Here's a classic bit that is always good for a laugh and is guaranteed to make the couple of your choice the life of your party.

Invite several couples to a party at your place and give all the same information as to date, time, etc. (If, from time to time, your crowd dresses formally for such gatherings, this would be a good occasion to request formal garb.) Now, single out one couple to inform that you are having a *costume* party. The rest of the joke practically takes care of itself.

For best results be sure not to invite people who are likely to discuss the party ahead of time with the couple to be victimized. Of course you could tip off the other guests about the "surprise," but the joke is much more effective if it hits them just as hard as your costumed friends.

Also, it's a good idea to tell the costumed couple that the party starts about a half-hour later than it actually does. That way everyone is sure to be on hand when the guests of honor ring the bell.

Yellowed
Journalism

We've already mentioned Hugh Troy and his genius for practical joking. Here is one of Troy's most clever stunts, which dates back to the mid-1930s but still works like a charm.

Like so many of Troy's gags, this one struck him out of the blue and, as was often his preference, the target was no one in particular—just anyone who dared cross his path. Troy was apparently walking down the street when his eye caught a tabloid with the big black headline: "ROOSEVELT WINS!" People were eagerly grabbing up the papers but only Hugh Troy would think to buy fifteen copies, take them all home and hide them in the closet for seven months.

When Troy was convinced a sufficient length of time had passed, he gathered up the old papers and enlisted the help of a number of friends to go with him to the New York subway. Not letting on that they knew one another, the gang boarded the train and sat throughout the car with the tabloid papers in front of them.

They spent the entire morning riding up and down the line, measuring the expressions of astonished passengers, who simply did not know what to make of the fact that everyone on the train was reading a paper with news that *they* thought was seven months old!

If you decide to try the old newspaper trick, here are a few things to keep in mind. Newspaper deteriorates quickly after it leaves the printing plant, so every effort must be made to preserve its fresh appearance. Best spot for storing: a cool, dark closet.

The other factor to remember is that the headline on your old copies must be big and bold so it catches people's attention. Most important, the headline—at least several months old when you use it—must involve something memorable and distinctive. After all, the headline "GASOLINE PRICES SOAR" will probably run tomorrow just as it did last year. On the other hand, if you and a dozen friends ride to work in a crowded bus reading papers with the headline "PATTY HEARST KIDNAPPED!" you are certain to raise a few eyebrows. You might even sell a few papers.

Bottoms Up!

Here's a little prank involving salt, pepper or sugar shakers—the glass kind with a metal screw-on top found in many restaurants.

The gag can be set up while the victim is away from the table, possibly at the bathroom. Begin by unscrewing the top of the shaker. Then place a piece of cardboard or plastic (a credit card will do) over the shaker and turn the whole thing upside down. Lower it to table level and slide the shaker onto the table, slowly removing the card so you spill as little as possible. Now you've got the shaker upside down on the table with nothing under it.

Slide it over to its proper place and put the cover of the shaker on what is now the top (but is really the bottom). Naturally, the cover won't screw on, but with most shakers it will just sit there as if screwed on.

People rarely pick up a shaker by the top; they reach for the middle. So when your dining partner returns and tries to lift the salt, pepper or sugar shaker, the result is sure to shake him up.

Does He
or Doesn't He?

A few years ago a bachelor friend of ours was entertaining a young lady who, while thumbing through a women's magazine, became interested in an ad for one of the nation's foremost mail-order emporiums of sleazy clothing.

Expressing an interest in a particular bra called Sexpose ("Bare your nipples . . . look natural . . . put your breasts on a shelf!"), she dialed the toll-free number to place an order. What she learned was that a phone order would not be filled until her check was received by mail and until that check cleared the bank. The entire coast-to-coast procedure could take a month. Was there any speedier method, she demanded. Yes, if she placed the order by using a major credit card, the merchandise would be sent out immediately. Unfortunately, the girl did not own a credit card—major or minor—and it was at this point that our male friend became the victim of a thoroughly unpremeditated practical joke. Not wishing to see his guest disappointed, he offered her the use of his credit card to order the bra. She happily used it but learned that the firm would only ship the goods to the name and address that appeared on the card. No matter; she could always pick up the package at her boyfriend's home.

That was three years ago. Our friend hasn't heard from the girl in some time (sure, she got her package but a few weeks later the romance fizzled). Yet hardly a month has gone by that he hasn't heard from the Hollywood mail-order outfit.

It seems this meticulous firm never fails to send catalog after catalog to anyone whose name has worked its way onto its list. Despite several letters of protest, the man continues to receive literature—all of which arrives unwrapped, with his name on it—heralding the latest colorful fashions that will "Flaunt your beauty" and allow you to "Go on, show off!"

When our friend's letters of protest didn't work, he tried casually mumbling to his mailman, "Gee, I can't understand why they keep sending me this stuff." But alas, he fears the comments to the mailman only made matters worse.

The point to all this is that magazines are chockablock with ads for unusual products and catalogs that you can have sent to some particularly deserving person. In some cases the firms require a dollar or so for their catalog, but that seems a small price to pay for some good fun. Besides, any mail-order company that gets hard cash from a buyer—even if it's only a buck—is sure to keep his name and address handy every time a new piece of literature rolls off the press.

And remember, it's the thought that counts.

The Invented Interview

The phony interview. It's one of the best ways to elicit laughs—and information—from someone who thinks he is about to get hired or accepted into college.

The team of Peter Funt and Steve North pulled this stunt with great precision on a fellow named Rick (not his real name) who had been talking nonstop for several years about wanting to go to U.C.L.A. for graduate work in filmmaking. The irony was that while Rick aspired to become a film producer, Steve was busy making films. And we began to suspect that Rick was including descriptions of Steve's work in his résumé. It is stuff like this that often prompts the most elaborate practical jokes.

We began by writing a letter to Rick, which we hoped he would believe was from the admissions people at U.C.L.A. For this we enlisted the aid of Mike Shatzkin, then a student at U.C.L.A. and always one to enjoy a good joke. Mike retyped our letter on school stationery and mailed it to Rick with the L.A. postmark. In essence, the letter said that a man from the film department would soon be in Denver for interviews and would like to speak to Rick about his work in film. Further, the note indicated a particular date and said Rick could expect a phone call from this Mr. Hoffstein that day.

Next step was to find someone to play the role of Mr. Hoffstein. We found the perfect man at the company where Steve's wife worked; he was in the personnel department. We also had printed a three-page questionnaire replete with leading questions such as: Describe five Super-8-millimeter movies you have personally produced in the last two years. Then we rented a small meeting room at a major hotel in Denver, which was to be the scene of the crime.

When the big day arrived, our "Mr. Hoffstein" phoned Rick and set up an afternoon appointment at the hotel. Then we gathered at the room to brief "Hoffstein" on the questions he should ask. We also advised the desk that we were conducting interviews for U.C.L.A.

Steve's wife, Barb, spent hours filling out phony questionnaires that could be left on the meeting table where Rick would be sure to see them. Meanwhile, we set up a tape recorder in the bathroom and hid a microphone in a folder on the table so that the entire session could be recorded. We also paid a young fellow $5 to wait with us in the room until Rick arrived and, pretending to have just finished an interview, mumble to Rick as he left, "Wow. I had no idea it was so tough to get into U.C.L.A.'s film school!"

To Rick's credit, he handled the hour-long interview quite well—so well, in fact, that while trying desperately to stifle our laughs in the bathroom, we began wishing we could actually get Rick into the damn school. On the other hand, he was pressured into a few moments of indiscretion and the whole thing was captured on tape.

The finale came that night. You see, we decided to let Rick leave the hotel still believing that the interview had been legit. We arranged to get together with him that evening at Barb and Steve's apartment to hear all about his much-awaited interview. So that night we sat and listened as Rick regaled us with the details until, when we could stand it no longer, Steve casually walked over to his tape machine and snapped it on. The results were so devastating that for several minutes Rick could not imagine what was happening. How had we managed to tape the interview (which he still believed was the real thing)? Only when we

54

produced the questionnaire he had filled out that afternoon did he begin to get the message.

Obviously, the phony interview has numerous possibilities which you can exploit with varying degrees of complexity among your co-workers or neighbors. As for Rick, he now owns a major movie theater; the rest of us, as you know, are still fooling with practical jokes.

Funny Money

It's an old bit—more a gag than a practical joke—but for some reason it never fails to get a great reaction.

It's the placing of a corner of a $10 or $20 bill (not a whole bill but just a snipped-off corner) under a book, ashtray or other object so it appears that a regular bill is sticking out from under the item. Just stand aside and watch the expressions on people who lift the object and discover nothing more than the small corner of the bill that was originally exposed. There was a time when the joke worked just as well with a $1 bill but, alas, inflation has made lifting an ashtray or whatever hardly worth the effort for a buck. Still, we've yet to encounter the person who can resist checking out what appears to be a "found" $10.

Another time-honored money gag involves gluing a thread or very thin clear plastic line to a bill, which is then left in a public spot, to be pulled away just as someone reaches for it. Last time we saw this tried was at a diner in Yonkers, New York, where the owner had a habit of using it as an initiation for new employees. With the boss standing out of view and holding the line, an employee noticed the $5 bill and tried to step on it. Just as he reached the bill, it was yanked a foot away. The guy shuffled over to step on it again, and before it dawned on him that someone was pulling his leg, he just about invented a new dance.

Still another funny money routine is to leave a quarter or half-dollar on a counter, table or the sidewalk. The catch is that you use the new super-glue to fasten the coin, then

57

watch the lengths to which most people will go to try and pry the coin loose.

One more. Find a spot where you are hidden from the view of passersby but can toss coins at their feet. Try it with nickels. Bounce the first coin close to the victim's feet and he will certainly stop to pick it up. As he begins to move away, drop another coin. Again he will stop, but this time will probably sneak a glance to see where the coins are coming from. How long the gag continues depends only on how much money you wish to invest because when it comes to time and patience, this is one joke where the "victim" is sure to have as much as you.

Calling All Suckers

He probably never realized it back in 1876, but Alexander Graham Bell's invention that year was perhaps the single best thing ever done to promote practical joking.

LADY: Hello.
CALLER: Is this the woman who washes?
LADY: Why no, it is not.
CALLER: Oh, you filthy thing!

"Hello, is Barney there?" asks a caller. "Sorry, you've got the wrong number," is the reply. "Hello, is Barney there?" asks a second caller. "Like I just told someone else, there's no such person here." "Hello, is Barney there?" ask a third, fourth, fifth and sixth caller, all of whom are told, "No!" So the seventh caller says, "Hello, this is Barney. Are there any messages for me?"

CALLER: Hello, tobacco shop, do you have Muriel in a box?
MAN: Yes, we do.
CALLER: Then you'd better let her out before she suffocates!

Or what about the woman who answered her phone and was told by an official-sounding sort of man that he was a phone repairman working on the lines in her neighborhood and planned some tricky wiring. Because he would be han-

dling "live" wires, she was cautioned not to use her phone under any circumstances for at least one hour. Sure enough, a few minutes later her phone starts to ring. And ring. And ring. And finally she can't stand it any longer and picks up the phone, only to hear a man scream, "Aaaaaaaaaaaah!"

CALLER: Hello, grocery store, do you have pig's feet?
WOMAN: Why yes, we do.
CALLER: Then how do you get your shoes on in the morning?

Call someone at random (or a friend or neighbor you wish to target who won't recognize your voice) and claim to be the phone company checking trouble on the line. Explain that it's a small problem involving voice modulation—have they noticed it? (Oh, sure.) Well, it can be fixed from the business office provided there is steady conversation on the line. For this, you point out, the company has a group of disabled former repairmen who sit home talking to people while the modulation is being adjusted. Explain that such a person will be calling shortly and the two should just keep talking until an operator breaks in to let them know the work is complete. Now call a second victim and say pretty much the same thing—except in this case explain that he should *place* a call to the special stay-at-home operator who will be glad to chat with him for as long as it takes. Give victim number two the phone number for victim number one and they do the rest.

YOU: We have a call from Washington. Will you take it?
THEM: Yes.
YOU: Then you must be nuts. He's been dead for years!

Again pretend to be the infamous phone repairman and tell people you will be "blowing out the lines" in their area during the next few hours. Don't skip a beat. Suggest they avoid using the phone if possible and might want to tie a bag or other protective covering over the phone receiver. Why? To catch the dirt and avoid a mess when the lines are blown out, of course!

61

Guaranteed Chilling Effects

There are countless pranks to be played with a substance that people usually do not come into contact with in their day-to-day lives—dry ice.

Dry ice is nothing more than solidified carbon dioxide. It's used regularly by television, film and stage producers to produce smoke or fog, which occurs when the product is placed in water. It is much colder than ordinary ice and cannot be touched with the bare hands. (To use it you must wear gloves made of heavy cloth; rubber or plastic gloves will fuse to the ice.)

Check the Yellow Pages for the nearest place to buy dry ice. We priced it at forty cents per pound (a one-pound chunk measures about five by twelve inches). The stuff will not last more than one day—even in your freezer—so you must purchase it on the day your stunt will be played.

Clouds of smoke can be produced by dumping dry ice in a swimming pool . . . in the tank or bowl of a toilet . . . in a glass (not to be used for drinking, only for showing) . . . in a watering can, etc. Because it is so cold, dry ice is also great for making Jell-O in unlikely places. Again, the bowl of a toilet is an ideal spot. You might also want to leave a three-inch layer of clear gelatin on the bottom of a bathtub.

There are plenty of uses for dry ice involving a car—someone else's. For example, if you were to place a pan of water with a slab of dry ice under the car—or better yet, under the hood or in the trunk—the clouds of smoke would certainly be noticed.

A woman we know managed to smuggle a chunk of dry
ice into a party and later dropped it into the punch bowl.
The hostess didn't know whether to call the bartender, the
fire department or a plumber.

The Season to Be Jolly

An all too humorless December ritual is the sending of Christmas and other seasonal cards. The joke, if there is one, is that many people compile long lists of those who send them cards and meticulously send cards in return—often checking to see that the cards are of equal value. Your office can add to the Christmas nightmare by issuing a list of names and addresses with the implication that cards should be sent to everyone, even if you have never met most of the people on the list. We know people who will not hesitate to send a card to someone whose name and address appears on the envelope of a card they receive, whether they know the person or not. The assumption is if someone sends us a card, we *must* know him.

If punching holes in this tradition appeals to you, here are a few suggestions. The easiest is to remail cards you've received to other people not acquainted with those whose names are on the cards. If you write the proper return addresses on the envelopes, there is a strong likelihood that these total strangers will wind up exchanging Christmas cards for years.

A different twist is to send a batch of cards to the people on your office mailing list but sign them all with the name of a co-worker who you are certain does not mail cards. The result will be that many people will send him cards even if they never intended to, and he might very well start sending cards after discovering how popular he is with the folks at the office.

Another suggestion is to single out one name on the office list and send a dozen or so cards to that person, all signed with the same name. Or how about adding this P.S. to a few cards: "Hope you enjoyed the wine."

If you have the patience, save all cards you receive this year and remail them next year. One method is to crudely scratch out the name at the bottom and sign someone else's. Another idea is to send last year's cards to people within your circle of friends so that they receive two cards from every member of the group. If they are true card fanatics, this twist is sure to drive them up their tree. They might consider it some new form of yule one-upsmanship and send out duplicate cards of their own!

By the Seat
of Their Chance

Some of the best practical jokes are those that thrust an unsuspecting male and female into a situation of enforced togetherness. Here we offer a number of setups that require only a bit of imagination and two tickets to a play or similar theatrical event.

The gist of the gag is that a pair of tickets is obtained, then one is given to the guy, the other to the girl, and they meet for the first time at the theater. The joke depends on what you tell—or don't tell—each of the victims.

1. Give one ticket to a girl and say it was an "extra"—but make no mention of a guy. Give the other ticket to a man and tip him off that you've given the other ticket to a girl at the office who is a nymphomaniac and can be turned on by blowing on her neck or in her ear.

2. Give one ticket to a male and say nothing. Give the other to a girl and explain that the guy sitting on her left is an old army pal who is very shy. Add that he's never had any experience with women, but if she would try to talk to him (without mentioning his army days), he would probably be glad.

3. Give one ticket to a girl and tell her that you gave the other ticket to a guy who is married with six kids and is always trying to fool around. Give the other to a guy and explain that the matching ticket went to a woman who is divorced and eager to meet someone new.

4. Give one ticket to a guy at the office and say you are fixing him up with a girl at the office who is secretly inter-

ested in him. Give the other ticket to a girl at the office and say exactly the same thing about the guy.

5. Buy three tickets. Give the center ticket to a girl and tell her nothing. Give the ticket on the girl's left to a guy and tell him you had *two* tickets and gave the other to a girl he's sure to like if he makes an effort to get to know her. Give the ticket on the girl's right to another guy and tell him exactly what you told the first guy.

6. Tell everyone who gets one of your tickets that you plan to be out of town for the next six months.

Picking on Knit-Pickers

There are people in this world who simply cannot avoid picking at a piece of lint or thread when it turns up on someone's sleeve. It is for these neatniks that the following piece of business is designed.

Pick up a small spool of thread, similar in size to the bobbin in a sewing machine, and as close as possible in color to the coat you will wear when the trick is played. Place the spool in the inside breast pocket of your coat and run the thread down the inside of your sleeve. Attach a sewing needle to the end of the thread and poke it through the fabric of the sleeve about three inches from the bottom of the cuff. Snip off the needle, leaving about two inches of thread hanging loose.

Now you are ready to confront your favorite knit-picker and wait for the inevitable tug at the thread. When you can see it coming, appear to be diverted so that the victim can pull heartily. The thread will just keep unreeling, of course. Only when the picker gives up do you "notice" what has happened. Then begin helping by pulling on the thread yourself. If you keep at it, you can "unravel" yards and yards from your coat.

A Real
Earful

Think about this: When you pick up the telephone, do you ordinarily look at the earpiece? Most people never do. And since the receiver sits upside down in the cradle, there is little chance that a foreign substance placed on the earpiece of a phone will ever be noticed.

We suggest peanut butter. Seriously, folks. There are those who prefer lampblack or a few dabs of Vaseline, but we think peanut butter works best.

The good thing about peanut butter is that when it is seen out of context—that is, out of the jar, out of the sandwich and out of the kitchen—it is easily mistaken for, well, other stuff that looks a lot like peanut butter when seen out of context. About the only way to be certain that what appears to be peanut butter *is* really peanut butter is to perform a taste test. But when there is a question about whether peanut butter is really peanut butter or some other stuff that looks like peanut butter, the last thing a person wants to try is a taste test.

Other interesting places to put peanut butter: on a doorbell, the bathroom light switch, the bottom of the cookie jar, in the mailbox, on the edge of a steering wheel facing the windshield.

Let the
Buyer Beware

Some call them "tag sales," others use the term "garage sales." You might remember the less attractive term "rummage sales." Whatever the name, the reference is to a process whereby strangers are invited to your home for the purpose of buying things you no longer wish to have around.

Good bit. But if you'd rather not have all those people traipsing through your home and if you happen to like all your possessions, why not arrange to have the sale at a neighbor's house? No need to bother him with the details. Simply pick the time and date and start tacking up signs to alert the public. It might even be a good idea to invest a few bucks for an ad in the local paper so that a large crowd is sure to attend.

Now, you're probably wondering what your neighbor is going to do on the day of the sale when people start knocking on his door. Most likely he will inform them they are mistaken, there is no sale. But what if you took the time to select a few items that are gathering dust in his house—say, the handmade guitar he only plays five or six times a week, or the canopy bed that his wife is always talking about, or his kids' electric trains. By mentioning those specific items in your advertising you increase the fun he's going to have. After all, when people come to the door inquiring about the Louis XIV table, what's he going to do, deny he owns it?

Naturally, you'll want to witness all the fun of such a sale. No problem. Just drop in, say you saw the ad, and offer to serve punch to the happy buyers. Who knows, maybe you will even go home with a great buy.

The Purr-fect Trick

Next time you are compelled to entertain a particular guest you would rather not fawn over, why not let your cats do it? Assuming, that is, that you own a cat or two.

The idea here is to provide a bit of recreation for your cats while at the same time convincing your guest that he has "quite a way with animals." All you need is catnip. Not the kind that is sewn into a cat's toy, but the loose catnip that is sold in most pet stores and looks like pot in a small plastic bag.

You will have to hide the catnip from your cats until it's time for the guest to arrive—and that, in itself, is quite a trick since cats have amazing investigatory powers when it comes to catnip. Best spot: the refrigerator. But be sure to move the stuff to the highest shelf in a closet an hour or so before the company arrives so it can warm to room temperature and reach maximum potency.

Now comes the only difficult part of the gag. As the targeted guest arrives, you must gather up a small handful of catnip and prepare to greet him at the door. Begin with a few pats on the back, then proceed to "brush" something off his clothing while actually applying as much catnip as you can without being too obvious. Fortunately, a little goes a long way.

Since catnip has no odor—as far as the human sense of smell is concerned anyway—your guest will never realize what's up. But your cats, you may be sure, will. As they begin to paw and nuzzle up to their new friend, you will, of course, remark about how rare it is for them to show such quick affection toward a visitor. The cats will become increasingly playful as their high builds; your guests, most likely, will soon grow tired of being the center of their attention. Just let cats and guest write the rest of the script.

If you don't happen to own a cat or two, you can perform a version of the gag by visiting someone who does. The best way to bring catnip on such an occasion is hidden in a gift for humans in the family. A lovely bouquet of flowers, thoroughly dusted with catnip, will promptly be torn to bits while your shocked hosts make excuses for their pets' odd behavior. Of course you can skip the gift and simply plant the catnip where it will do the most good. Pick a spot—such as under the pillows on the couch—where nothing will get broken in the scramble. Then just watch the felines drive everyone up the wall.

Hearing Is
Believing (or Is It?)

When E. F. Hutton talks (if commercials are to be believed), people listen. With that in mind, try this.

At a suitably crowded place—such as a restaurant or elevator—strike up a preplanned conversation with a friend in which you reveal a hot stock market tip or a sure thing at the racetrack. For example, you might talk about how you've just spent your life savings on stock in Acme Aerospace because your uncle, who works there, happened to be in the president's office when NASA called to confirm that Acme won the contract for the space shuttle. Similarly, you can pretend to discuss the $1,000 bet you have just placed on Speed Queen because your uncle, who works at the track, learned that the horse was fed some illegal pep pills and is sure to run like hell in tonight's feature.

A woman we know used to pull a gag like this at the office. Rather than stage a conversation with a partner, she preferred to work alone by letting people in the office overhear her telephone conversations (which were actually placed to the recorded weather report). She would gab nonstop about anything the snoops nearby might be tempted to believe: "Joan, did you hear that Mr. Franklin [head of the company] was arrested last night for drunk driving?" "Yes, Annie, they say we're going to have a foot of snow. I've canceled all my weekend plans." "Rhoda, would I lie to you? Yes, they're testing the air conditioners in my office for Legionnaire's Disease!" "So anyway, Barb, I don't care if the new district manager here does look like Robert Redford.

Now that I know he's got a wife and two kids, I'm certainly not going out with him." "What? Dee, you say they put *what* in the water cooler? You're kidding! Listen, let me call you back later. I think someone might be trying to hear what we're saying . . ."

Fit
to be Tied

Although the art of practical joking has all but disappeared from most segments of American society, it remains alive and well on the college campus. Everything from the short-sheeted bed to balloons filled with water are still part of growing up at college. But for those of you who would rather not grow up just yet, here's an oldie but goody.

The basic bit is to tie a door shut with rope so the person on the inside can't get out. In college dorms the routine usually involves tying a doorknob to the one directly across the hall. Often the gag is timed to some critical event like, say, the delivery of a pizza to the front desk, which, of course, the victim waits an hour for and then discovers he cannot get out of his room to receive.

Recently the old rope-on-the-door trick was resurrected in grand style in a Manhattan apartment building. The man behind the gag went to great lengths (of rope) to tie all the doors in one particular hallway together. This was done by looping the rope around each doorknob up one side of the hall and down the other. The rope was left slightly slack so that the doors could be opened about six inches—but no more. To set off the chain reaction, the joker went down to the front door of the building at 6 A.M. and rang the intercom for each apartment. That served to rouse everyone. A few minutes later he ran down the hall and rang all the doorbells. Not only were the folks shocked to discover they were roped in to their apartments, but every time one of them tried to yank his door open, he tightened the rope, thereby slamming the door in his neighbor's face. This tug-of-war continued for about twenty minutes until finally the superintendent came up and cut them loose.

The guy never did tell us whether he admitted the joke when it was over. We presume he never mentioned it; with all that rope around, there's no telling what those people might have done.

The Seeds of Astonishment

One of the funniest *Candid Camera* gags involved a potted plant placed between two tables in a restaurant. Right before the patrons' eyes, it began growing—to an enormous height!

As with many of the bits on the TV show, the mechanics of this one are too complicated for making it work in your home. The plant was made to "grow" through an elaborate setup involving a member of the production staff hiding beneath the table and pushing the plant up through a special pot. But don't despair. You, too, can achieve results every bit as funny on your own.

A woman we know used a more subtle technique: She bought three plants in identical pots, as close in appearance as possible, except that their sizes could be described as small, medium and large. She placed the small plant in a prominent spot on her coffee table and hid the other two in the bathroom. While entertaining a small group of friends, she casually brought out a watering can and gave the plant a drink. "Don't we look thirsty," she said to the plant in the best spirit of talking to one's green-leafed friends.

While the visitors were in the kitchen enjoying dinner, the hostess slipped out and switched the small plant for the medium one. Needless to say, when the guests returned to the living room—having had a few drinks with their meal—they wondered to themselves about the apparent "growth" of the plant. The difference in size, mind you, was not great,

so although the guests were troubled by this matter, they preferrred not to mention it.

Later in the evening the woman served bowls of mixed nuts and popcorn to her friends and, ever so casually, sprinkled a few nuts at the base of the plant, remarking that her plants "just love *people* food on special occasions as a *treat*."

Toward the end of the evening, the guests moved to the den to view some color slides, allowing the woman an opportunity to make the final switch. When she put the largest of the three plants on the coffee table, she carefully placed a few bits of nuts in the pot, as sort of "leftovers."

Needless to say, the guests were agape when they returned to the living room. A few were finally moved to comment on the increased size of the plant, but the woman just shrugged it off as nothing out of the ordinary. Having planted the seeds of astonishment, she was free to sit back and enjoy the fruits of her labor.

Leave 'Em
in Stitches

All you need to have for this gag is a needle and thread; and all you need to do is get into someone's pants.

Actually, it's more innocent than it sounds. It's a sure-fire way to confound someone by sewing across the middle of his pants pocket. The effect of the gag is to make the pocket smaller, almost like the time-honored gag of short-sheeting a bed. (For the uninitiated, short-sheeting is as basic to summer camp, military camp or college campus life as raising the flag in the morning. It is done by making a bed with one sheet instead of two and extending the single sheet halfway down the mattress, then folding it back. Once a blanket is placed on top, the bed appears to be made properly until someone tries to get between the sheets and his feet are stopped midway by the fold.)

With a pocket you achieve a similar effect by stitching right across it, halfway in. When the wearer stuffs in his hand, he finds the pocket has shrunk. This can be done with a coat or any garment on which the pocket hangs free inside.

Another stitching gimmick is to sew up a buttonhole. This should be done with thread that matches the shirt or blouse and is best worked on one of the holes in the center of the garment. A variation that requires a bit more work is to sew your victim's buttons—all of them—right over the buttonholes. To do this you must remove the buttons from one side of a shirt and sew them over the buttonholes with a stitch that closes the holes as well. (Note that the button

itself hides the hole.) Or, if the shirt has plain white buttons that are easy to match, you might want to sew a duplicate set over the buttonholes rather than remove any buttons. This way, the wearer finds he has two complete rows of buttons—but not a single buttonhole.

If you're into sewing, you can always pick up a label from the discount store in your community and sew it on top of the label of your spouse's designer suit, coat or scarf. If it goes unnoticed at home, pick a "nice" time to bring it to everybody's attention at a party with, "Is this a Dior or Halston?" while deftly exposing the undesirable label.

A final bit of needlework. Men's undershorts have a folded opening in the front for easy access when . . . well, for easy access. You might just want to sew that opening closed for the husband or lover you'd like to get a rise out of.

Fastest Catsup
in the West

As everyone knows, you can't get catsup out of a bottle without giving it a dozen raps on the bottom. Usually all that pounding results in only a slow trickle of catsup, so there is little risk of flooding your hamburger by hitting the bottle too hard. But what if there were a way to rig an ordinary catsup bottle so that at first nothing came out . . . then after a few pounds a tiny bit came out . . . then, finally, after heavy pounding, the entire contents poured out all at once like water from a busted pipe? Where there's a will, there's a way.

Naturally, you'll need a bottle of catsup. It should be nearly empty; if not, you must pour the contents into some other container. (If you experience difficulty in getting the catsup out, just pound on the bottom of the bottle.) Next, mix a batch of catsup-looking liquid by adding a bit of real catsup to a lot of tomato juice. Pour the mixture into the catsup bottle, filling it to just below the base of the neck.

Now you must construct a "plug" for the neck of the bottle. Several materials work well for this purpose, such as ordinary dough (colored red by mixing it with catsup) or even peanut butter (fast becoming the practical joker's favorite food). The trick is to make the plug thick enough to hold back the flow of the tomato juice mixture, but thin enough so that several good bangs on the bottle will cause the plug to give way. When the plug is placed in the neck of the bottle, it is completely hidden from view by the label that circles the neck.

85

Finally, put a few spoons of real catsup on top of the plug. In this way, the victim will see a full bottle and will get a little bit of real catsup when he starts pouring it on his plate. When the flow stops, he will start pounding. When the dike breaks, there will be no stopping the tomato juice from gushing forth.

The Greatest
Story Ever Told

A favorite party game involves creating a simple story that one guest must figure out by asking a series of questions. For those who have never played, it goes like this: Each guest gets a turn to be the questioner and leaves the room while the rest of the group works out the plot to a short story. When the player returns, he may use only questions that can be answered yes or no in trying to unravel the yarn.

Okay. After your group has been playing the game for a while, try this amusing little twist. When one guest is out of the room believing a new story is being plotted, the group agrees that this time the story will be that *there is no story*. Instead the players will answer yes or no to questions in such a way that the victim actually concocts a story as he goes along. From time to time the players will ask for a recap and marvel at how well this one player is divining the plot.

To enhance the effect, the rest of the group should pretend to argue as to whether certain questions deserve a yes or no answer. Play this trick on the right person and you might wind up with a regular "Gullibles' Travels"!

Two Cokes in the Side Pocket

A guy walks into a diner, orders a couple of Cokes to take out, pays for them . . . then matter-of-factly pours both into the side pocket of his coat, says, "They're easier to carry this way," and walks out.

A woman is ready to leave the table at a restaurant and comments to her date and the waiter that she hardly touched her fruit compote. Without hesitation, she spills the entire dessert into her pocket, smiles and leaves.

It's a very effective sight gag. The trick, obviously, is either a very messy pocket or a plastic lining inside the pocket. The poor man's version is a plastic sandwich bag tucked into the pocket in advance and taped to the sides so it will stay open. The luxury version is a hot water bottle cut in half and sewn into the pocket.

We know a chap who tried this gag and got several laughs. A few of the laughs were at a restaurant when he poured a bowl of mushroom soup into his pocket. The rest of the laughs came when he bent over to get into a cab and spilled most of the soup on his pants.

An Engaging Gag

Every young lady looks forward to the day when her local newspaper carries the happy news of her wedding engagement. But just how much joy she will find in a story about an engagement that does not exist is something you can only determine by carrying out this prank.

Major newspapers in the nation's big cities have learned the hard way that all press releases must be thoroughly checked. Still, there are scores of understaffed papers in smaller communities that will print just about anything they receive in the mail as long as it looks legit. You will have to determine which category your local paper fits into before bothering to send it the phony announcement about the man and woman you'd most like to see wedded in print.

Type your announcement—doubled spaced—on white paper. It should read something like this:

> Mr. and Mrs. Paul Gabriel Bennotti of Upper Saddle River, N. J., and St. Maarten, the Netherlands Antilles, have announced the engagement of their daughter, Tara Ann Fusco Bennotti, to David Chalmers Millstein, son of Dr. and Mrs. James C. Millstein of New Milford, Conn. A wedding is planned in September.
>
> Miss Bennotti, an aspiring actress, received a bachelor's degree from Paxton University in North Conway, N. H. Her father was Mayor of Jonesboro, Ark.
>
> Mr. Millstein plans to attend classes at Hunter College next fall. He is presently employed as overnight

90

manager of the McDonald's restaurant in Strafford-Wayne, Pa. His father is a lawyer in Manhattan and his mother, Murial Chalmers, is a sculptor in Norton, Mass.

You can make your "facts" about the couple as valid or fictional as you wish. But resist the temptation to include more than basic biographical information because that will arouse the curiosity of your local society editor.

Service Maid
to Order

Imagine how surprised your guests would be if they came for dinner at your home and found that you had hired a maid and/or butler for the occasion. Better yet, imagine their surprise if the "help" gradually wrecks the party by becoming increasingly clumsy and rude.

This routine has been tried in numerous ways over the years and it works best if you tailor it to your own situation. Basically, the idea is to enlist the help of a man or woman or both to play the parts of butler and/or maid at your party. They should plan in advance with you what pattern their "service" should follow.

Be sure that things start slowly so the guests become comfortable with this special treatment. Arrange for things to go wrong gradually. If you're willing to play along, a good start would be a bowl of soup dumped in *your* lap. (Yes, the soup could be spilled on one of your guests instead but, frankly, that's not the idea of the joke. Better that you prepare by wearing something that can take it and making sure that your "soup" is mostly water. When the liquid winds up in your lap, the guests will never suspect you planned it that way.)

Let the soup incident set off an exchange of insults between you and your servants. Act embarrassed and try to cut short the arguing while your maid and butler carry on. Next, one of the servants should spill something else in the center of the table. Again, none of the guests is affected, but

93

the party is clearly going to hell. If any of the guests makes
a remark, have the help ready to shoot back an insult.

You take it from there. How far you want to go depends
on your own group's tolerance for this kind of put-on. You
might plan an ending in which the servants walk out in
disgust. Or, you could pretend to patch things up by inviting the maid and butler to sit down and enjoy the rest of the
meal with you and your guests—leaving everyone to wonder what to make of the two newcomers now stuffing themselves at the table while you do the serving.

All
Strung Out

If you ever see someone approaching you on the street with a big ball of string and an even bigger grin, watch out. His plan may be to rope a dope.

The gag is a classic. Get some string or twine—any kind will do—and mosey down the street till you find the right pigeon. Explain to this person that you are supposed to be surveying the area but are having a difficult time since your assistant took ill and left you alone. Would he mind giving you a hand? Actually, a hand is all you need—to hold one end of the string while you make the measurements. Then, while your new helper keeps a firm grip on the string, you back away, unrolling more string as you go. When you come to the end of the block, wave and nod that all is going well and turn the corner.

Continue unrolling the string until you reach the end of the ball. Now stand and wait for another helpful stranger to come along. Explain that you are having a difficult time with a survey, etc. Would he mind holding this piece of string while you run around the corner to measure at the other end? Fine.

Take in a movie.

The Locked
Vest Monster

A small dime-store padlock is all you need to pull off a bit of mischief that will confound your victim and leave you holding the key to his peace of mind.

Your prank must be worked in a coatroom, closet, hallway or other spot where those you live or work with hang their coats. The object is to attach the padlock to the buttonhole of the victim's garment in such a way that it is rendered useless or strangely misshapen.

For example, if you lock the victim's coat to the coat rack itself, it is not likely that he will be able to remove it until you provide the key. But rather than be so malicious, you might choose to lock the coat to a hanger, meaning that it can still be worn but not without arousing the curiosity of everyone your victim passes on the way home. Even more subtle is the notion of locking the buttonhole to another buttonhole—on someone else's coat. Or, you can lock one buttonhole on the victim's coat to the buttonhole just above or below it on the same garment. This will surely confuse the wearer since the padlock provides just an awkward bulge.

You undoubtedly will find other uses for the padlock gimmick if you let your imagination run wild. As for ending the bit, we've found that one of the most amusing methods is to slip the key in a little-used pocket of the very coat you have padlocked. The inside breast pocket of a man's coat would be an ideal hiding place. Another approach involves sending the key to the victim's home through the mail. You

97

might want to drop the key in the mail the day before you work the trick. This way, your victim will ride home with a heavy wooden hanger locked to the front of his coat, only to find the key waiting mysteriously in his mailbox. A different twist is to mail the key *two days* before you go to work so that it arrives *before* the gag is tried. Obviously, your victim will have no idea what the key is for and therefore will never think of bringing it with him to the office; its use will only dawn on him when he finds his coat locked up.

We tried the latter version of the joke and sent the key in a letter along with this message:

> This letter contains, as you can see,
> A strange and un-solicited key.
> What it's for we cannot say,
> But please don't throw our gift away.
> Just view this key as an antidote,
> For the illness soon to strike your coat!

Where There's Smoke, There's . . .

No doubt about it, this is a childish prank that should only be played on one's worst enemies by one who never seems to grow up.

Sometimes it's done with a brown paper bag, other times with a folded newspaper. In either case, the idea is to put something inside the bag—or between the folds of the paper—something like, oh, rotten eggs. (Ever notice how books like this mention rotten eggs as if they are something most people have sitting around the house? Never mind. Use fresh eggs if that's all you have and rest easy that they will be rotten by the time the trick is over.)

With your bag or paper filled with eggs, you visit your victim's front door and place the gift on the mat. Next, set fire to the bag (newspaper), and as soon as you are certain it is burning well, ring the doorbell and take off. Naturally, your friend will answer the door, see the fire, and try to stamp out the flames with his foot . . . leaving him with a footful of whatever you put in the bag (or paper).

Instead of eggs, you might consider using a large quantity of peanut butter. The reasoning is detailed elsewhere in a gag called "A Real Earful."

A Simple Game
of Tag

How about the man (or woman) who struts around the office in too-fancy clothes and is always making much ado about his appearance, which to you is nothing?

Undoubtedly, the best way to deal with him would be to provide a set of the emperor's new clothes—but since that gag has not been perfected yet, try this one. Search the racks of a "bargain basement" store in your city for some labels or tags that read "Irregular" or "Factory Second" or "Final Clearance" or something like that. Unless you know someone at the store, or actually shop there yourself, you're going to have to steal a couple of these tags. No need to worry, though; most stores are concerned about losing their shirts, not the tags on them. (Make sure they're not the thick plaster tags that set off store alarms.)

Next thing you should get is one of those special wire clips attached to clothes when they come back from the dry cleaners. It's shaped like a figure-eight so that when you squeeze one end, the other spreads open. When you let go, the clip snaps shut.

After attaching the tag to the clip, you are ready to come up behind your victim and carefully attach it to his or her coat, skirt, trousers, whatever. Pickpockets, you know, pretend to bump into their victim as they strike—try it, if you like. The idea is to have this peacock parading through the office all day with your gag tagging behind.

The tag bit brings to mind the old schoolyard trick of slapping someone on the back while sticking him with a

sign that says "Kick Me" or something similarly creative.

Actually, this is still a funny gag if properly updated. Let's say you happen to know where your colleague has been spending his free time lately. There's no reason why you can't slap him on the back, leaving a sticker that says, "Ask me what I was doing last night at the Holiday Inn."

Finder's Weepers

We first learned of this gag in college—not from the students, but from one crotchety old professor who apparently popped his suspenders the day a much younger man was chosen over him as head of the geophysics department.

Seems the old guy had quite a collection of dusty, out-of-date textbooks, many of them duplicates. One day he asked a local printer to prepare a batch of labels that could be glued inside the books. The labels said that this was a rare and valuable book, and if lost, the owner would pay a substantial reward for its safe return. Below that the label had the name and address . . . not of the professor who actually owned the worthless books, but of the whippersnapper who ran the geophysics department.

It should be clear by now that the next step was to paste the labels in dozens of the old books, then carefully "lose" them all over the campus and the surrounding community. One can imagine the reaction of the young scholar when a parade of students came to his door expecting a reward for books they had found. And one can further imagine what form of retaliation the students devised after being told there was no reward.

Objects other than books can be used with equal success, and while a printed reward notice is best, a carefully handwritten version will probably work too.

We learned the story quite by accident. The old goat who pulled the trick became afflicted with the same phobia that strikes many practical jokers—fear that for some reason

the gag is not working. He decided to paste labels in a few additional books and hired a student to take them to the address listed and claim the reward. Unfortunately, the student became suspicious and demanded to know the truth. The old teacher told him the story in return for a promise of secrecy. And that's how things stood until now, when the student published the trick in his book about practical jokes.

Better Than
Greasy Kids' Stuff

As every practical joker knows, certain things look very much like other things and can easily be confused, often with funny results. Certain brands of soap, for example, can be sliced to look just like certain types of cheese. Salt looks like sugar, shaving cream is a dead ringer for whipped cream, and everyone knows the many uses of peanut butter.

But what about motor oil? This valuable liquid is rarely seen—especially by women—outside the can or away from the car. We've discovered that motor oil can very convincingly pass for shampoo! Try emptying a bottle of baby shampoo or any castile variety and filling the bottle with oil. It is virtually impossible to see that a switch has been made, yet the trick will quickly become clear when someone hops in the shower and starts rubbing the stuff into his scalp. Also, because of its silky consistency oil can double for hand cream or lotion. It's perfectly harmless but gives the user a distinctive Joe's Garage odor that is harder to get rid of than it is to acquire.

We learned of the motor oil bit from a woman who spent the better part of a marriage hounding her husband about the foul smell that followed him around all weekend after he worked on his car or lawn mower. Finally, she pulled the shampoo switch and he got the message. It goes to show that in the world of practical joking—where there's a way, there's a will.

The
Missing Meal

Whenever you throw a party your guests are easy targets for a good practical joke. After all, they are likely to be on their best behavior and, as a group, will probably endure more abuse than they might individually under different circumstances.

A few years ago we slipped into a circle of friends who fancied themselves gourmets and enjoyed rotating the honor of inviting the group to their homes for dinner. After being a part of this for a while, we decided to have a little fun with our somewhat stuffy bunch and set about preparing what we called "the missing meal."

The idea was to create a fabulous feast, served on the best china on a lavishly decorated table. It was, truly, a gourmet's delight, except that each course was strangely devoid of its prime ingredient.

We began with shrimp cocktail. Each guest was given an ornate goblet overflowing with crisp lettuce, a delightful shrimp sauce and other garnish—but no shrimp. The gag was off to a great start with priceless expressions around the table as one guest after another poked in vain for a piece of shrimp. But as we expected, no one said a word. We assume they thought the shrimp had been inadvertently left out of their portion; perhaps they attributed it to an economy measure prompted by the high cost of seafood, or maybe they believed this was a new shrimpless shrimp cocktail.

The main course was billed as Kentucky beef stew. It was

chock-full of delicious vegetables and actually tasted like beef stew because we cooked it with beef but carefully plucked out all pieces before the dish was served. Why call it "Kentucky" stew? Well, we figured it sounded good and might further confuse the guests. After all, who would question the content of Kentucky beef stew when doing so might reveal ignorance of this classic early American dish.

The dessert was best of all. It was a hefty banana cream pie with no shortage of cream but a marked absence of bananas. (We decided to include a few shots of banana flavoring just to add credibility to our otherwise incredible meal.) In a way, our pie resembled the item served at many fancy diners and delies—a good four inches of cream piled on a layer of crust, but not much else.

You might try doing even more with the gag. How about rum punch without rum, or puff pastry hors d'oeuvres with nothing in the puffs?

If you don't happen to be part of a gourmet society, you might want to plan such a meal for the neighbors. Rather than serve everyone a "missing meal," it is sometimes appropriate to single out one guest for the special treatment. Be careful, though, not to make his or her plight too obvious at first; the gag works best when it builds throughout the meal.

Equally good targets are the relatives who always happen to drop by at dinnertime yet never seem to reciprocate with dinner invitations. But watch out: People who mooch a meal are always the first to complain when it appears you are not giving them their money's worth.

Classified
Information

The vaudeville comedian used to say, "Every morning before I get up I read the obituary column in the newspaper. If my name's not listed, I feel okay."

These days some people are almost that paranoid about their jobs—they check the classified sections daily to see if they are about to be replaced or to find out who else is getting the ax.

Classified sections of newspapers are perfect for gags because the paper rarely checks your facts, just your payment. Taking advantage of this condition, a classic ruse was to run an ad that said, "Last chance to send your dollar to . . ."and then gave an address. The money would pour in.

There's no reason why you can't put someone at the office into a dither by running an ad for his job. A guy we know ran such an ad for his supervisor's job, and to add insult to injury, posted a notice about the job on the company bulletin board the same morning that the ad appeared in the paper. The trick became the hottest topic of discussion at the office, and the guy responsible for it could not resist taking credit. Just two weeks later he thought someone else was using his material when he noticed in the paper an ad almost identical to the one he had placed for the job of supervisor. Unfortunately, this was a *real* ad, for another su-

pervisory position in the same company. After hearing gossip about the trick, the company execs passed over our friend for this job and gave it to an outsider.

Moral: When it comes to practical joking . . . it's the squeaky wheel that gets screwed.

Wrong Number Please

Consider this: When someone dials your phone by mistake and drags you away from whatever you are doing, perhaps late at night, how much courtesy does he deserve? Not much, we warrant.

Perhaps the easiest thing to do—especially if the caller is someone you know has made this mistake before—is to say, "Hold on, please," and put down the phone and leave it down until the caller withers away on the other end.

On the other hand, if the caller is asking for a particular person, you can act a bit nervous and say, "Gee, I'm afraid . . . uh, he's kind of busy right now . . . I mean he's, uh, talking to someone, uh . . . listen, why don't I have him call you back?"

The key to mistreating people who call you accidentally is to have your mind set ahead of time that you intend to fix their wagon. That way, you won't hesitate or be caught by surprise.

If they are calling a business establishment, you should be prepared to take the call and answer the questions. Does the caller want to make an appointment? Sure, what time? Do we have fresh flounder? Sorry, not today. Is your dry cleaning ready yet? Well, there seems to have been a bit of a mistake down at the plant, maybe we'd better tell you about it when you drop by.

But there is an even bigger nemesis than the person who calls the wrong number and that's the character who calls

114

the right number—yours!—to try and sell you something. This person should always be taught a lesson.

Again, the easiest thing to do is say, "Hold on," and leave the phone while you watch at least a half-hour of TV. Or, you might want to play the salesperson along but apologize and put the phone down every thirty seconds.

Another ploy is to pretend to try and sell the caller something. Tell him you happen to be a used car salesman and you can give him a great deal on a '72 T-Bird. When he tries to slip back into his pitch, start explaining what great condition the car is in.

One important thing to keep in mind is that some phone sales organizations have house rules for their callers stating they may not give up until you say no two or three times. This is frequently how newspaper and magazine sales people are trained. If that's the case, you can chew the caller's ear off for a half-hour talking about your dog's new puppies, etc., just so long as you don't say the secret word: "No!"

"For Hotel Use Only"

We have mentioned a number of gags that are appropriate for the hosts of a party to try on their guests. Here is a very effective bit that the guests can use to turn the tables.

The only preparation necessary is to abscond with a towel and wrapped bar of soap from a hotel. (For many folks that is not a chore but standard operating procedure.) Keep in mind that the items you lift must bear the name of the hotel—as prominently as possible—as most offered in hotel bathrooms do. You might even want to pick up a box of tissues from the hotel if you can find the kind that is clearly marked "For Hotel Use Only."

These items should be hidden in a coat, pocketbook or other convenient place when going to the party. Shortly after arriving, ask to use the bathroom, and once inside, switch your hotel towel, soap and other paraphernalia for the things provided by your hosts. (Remember that the wrapper should be left on the bar of hotel soap; it looks better that way and forces the next person to take note of the hotel name.) Hide the things you have removed in a hamper or other spot out of view (if necessary, take them out with you).

As already acknowledged, most normal people steal things from hotel bathrooms. But few people like everyone to know about it, which is what will happen to your hosts when other guests use the john.

She Snoops
to Conquer

A frequent frustration at the office: the snooping secretary who you suspect spends her time rummaging through the things on your desk when you're not around.

Teach her a lesson by taking a sheet of company stationery, folding it in half and typing on the outside: "Confidential." Inside, you write a personal message to her, such as:

> Good morning, Miss Jones. I'll be in a little later than usual today but there's really no need to tidy up my desk, I can do it myself.

Needless to say, your personal message is sure to shock the devil out of Miss Jones. There is one problem. You know that after reading the note, Miss Jones will carefully put it back where she found it and never dare mention it to you. This will take the wind out of your sails as a practical joker unless you find a way to prove that the trap has been sprung.

It might be as simple as a smile. Next time you greet her, say nothing about the trick but flash a knowing smile. She might just fall apart before your eyes. But to be guaranteed of personal satisfaction, you can always use an old *Mission Impossible* device. After placing the note on your desk exactly where you want it, pluck a single hair from your head and put it inside the folded note. She will never notice the hair, but if it's gone when you return to the office, you will know the trick worked.

Tanks
for Nothing!

As we enter the era of buck-a-gallon gas, more and more motorists are becoming sensitive about gasoline prices and gasoline mileage. And you're sure to know at least one motorist who has purchased a small foreign car recently and can't stop talking about the great mileage he's getting.

There is a marvelous way to handle this guy; it takes some time and patience but is well worth the effort. Begin by obtaining a gas can and siphon. You must also have easy access to the victim's car—preferably at night—perhaps on the street, in his driveway, or in an unlocked garage.

For the first week of the gag, you merely *add* a bit of gas to the tank each night. Begin with, say, half a gallon and gradually increase the dose each night so that by week's end you are contributing about two gallons to your neighbor's tank. The effect of your efforts will be apparent each day in the comments of your victim, who will undoubtedly increase his boasting about the super mileage he is getting. Why not. Thanks to you, he actually is getting more miles to the gallon than the EPA people ever dreamed possible when they rated his car.

Now, just as gradually, you reverse the process. Each night you reduce the amount of gas you donate to his tank until, finally, you are not adding any. By this time, the victim is beginning to worry about his car. Let it go for a few days. Then, return to his car by night and gradually begin *removing* gas with the siphon. Each night remove more than the night before.

Pretty soon your target—the guy with the brand-new foreign car that was getting great mileage—is sure his car is falling apart. Of course, he won't be so eager to brag about mileage but you might ask how he's doing. And imagine the reaction he'll get when he returns to his dealer to complain about the way his car now eats gas. "I swear," he's likely to say, "just two weeks ago I was getting fifty, maybe sixty, miles per gallon!"

Bits and Pieces,
Pieces of Bits

Here are a few quickies to keep in mind for a rainy day (or a perfectly sunny day that you would like to make just a bit dreary).

—Find a key identical in appearance to one on a friend's key chain and make a switch.

—Remove the license plate from someone's car and bolt it back on upside down.

—Send out invitations to a "24-caret dinner." Then serve each guest a dish with 24 carrots.

—Take this week's *TV Guide*, and using the method described in "Under Cover Assignment" (see page 15), put last week's listing section in this week's editorial section.

—Check someone's coat to see if it has a lining. If so, cut a hole in a pocket so things "disappear" into the lining.

—"Borrow" your neighbor's camera when it's left in the drawer with half the roll exposed and snap a single picture of one unusual part of your wife's anatomy. Then replace the camera and wait till your neighbor sees what develops.

—When treated poorly by a waiter, leave his tip in the water glass. Better yet, turn the glass upside down on a

menu or other flat object, then slide it onto the table with the water and tip still inside.

—Have someone paged at a restaurant or airport. If, for example, you know he's single and out with his girl friend, have the page say, "Please call your wife."

—Using thin green wires, attach a few apples to your neighbor's cherry tree. Or try strawberries on his watermelon plants. Or tomatoes.

—Circulate a memo at the office in the late morning that gives everyone the afternoon off.

—Tip a highway worker $5 to dump his truckful of snow in your neighbor's driveway. Or "reshovel" his walk by yourself.

—Take apart something big—like a piano or an old car—and reassemble it in someone's room while he or she is away for the weekend.

—Remove a stack of tissues from the box and carefully glue them all together with just a dab of glue. Then replace them in the box fan-fold style so the next time someone starts pulling they all come out in a string.

—Put some paprika in a guy's electric shaver so when he empties it he will wonder how badly he's been scratching his face.

—Drop a hint to someone that the office staff wants to give him a twelve-volume set of travel books as a gift. Then arrange for everyone to give him volume one.

—When your guest's umbrella is standing tip-down in

124

the umbrella rack, pour confetti or rice between the folds. When he opens it he'll be in the "rain."

—After being served a meal on a plane, dump it into one of the air sickness bags. When the stewardess walks by, make a face and eat out of the bag.

—Gift-wrap some household garbage and leave the package on your boss's desk. Or leave the "gift" in a public place—perhaps a bus station—where it's sure to be stolen.

—Retype a few cards in the office Rolodex so that certain important people are listed next to certain unimportant numbers.

—Fill someone's room with wadded-up newspaper (really *fill* it, right to the ceiling) so he can barely open the door.

—If someone's bedroom door opens inward, tape newspaper over the entire outside door frame, then call that person for dinner.

—If someone's bedroom door opens outward, tape newspaper over the entire inside door frame, then wait till he gets home.

—Using a straight pin or sewing needle, poke a hole in a banana, then twist the pin from side to side so that you cut through the fruit without increasing the size of the hole in the peel. Repeat this down the entire banana, making holes about a quarter-inch apart. When someone peels the banana, he will not notice the tiny pinholes but will be shocked to find the entire fruit presliced!

—Collect a dozen houseflies or other bugs. Drop one in

each section of an ice tray and place in the freezer till cubes are needed.

—Next time you are seated at one end of a long table— say, in a noisy cafeteria—prearrange a signal with someone at the other end. At the signal, you turn to Ralph (the unknowing person seated next to you) and say, "Tom wants you." At the same moment, your confederate at the other end turns to Tom (the unknowing person seated next to him) and says, "Ralph wants you."

—Buy another copy of this book. Wrap it in brightly colored paper so it looks like a gift and send it to someone!

The Used
Tree Bit

WANTED—USED CHRISTMAS TREES. TOP PRICES PAID. BRING TO 1245 SOUTH PEARL STREET, NOON TO 5 P.M. TODAY.

Imagine seeing that ad in the classified section of your newspaper about seven or eight days after Christmas. Even if you had no idea what "top prices" were for used Christmas trees, you would probably conclude that it's more than you had planned on getting for yours—and off you would go.

That's the gag. Find a Scrooge-like character in your neighborhood who deserves the worst and run the ad for one day with his address. By all means, drop by for a look at the action and, if you celebrate Christmas, bring your tree.

We think Christmas trees fit this gag quite well. But if you are eager to try it at other times of the year, use your own imagination in finding the item to advertise the need for. How about cardboard boxes . . . or freshly-cut but not yet dried-out grass . . . or used aluminum siding.

Peter's
Favorite

After reading this gag, give it a bit of extra thought. Picture it. We think this is one of the most effective practical jokes to come along because it includes all the elements that a good gag should have. It is harmless; relatively inexpensive, workable by just one person and, most important, sets up an incredible dilemma for the victim.

Your target should be anyone's home or office that you can gain access to for about ten minutes. You will need a child's inflatable wading pool, plenty of water and several quarts of grape juice. You must work the gag in a room that has no outlet (door, window, etc.) any wider than the pool will be when fully inflated.

Place the wading pool in this room, blow it up to maximum size, and dump in the water and juice—the liquid must fill the pool right to the top. That's it. You have constructed an obstacle that looks harmless yet is almost as impossible to move as a crate of live alligators.

Exactly what is your friend going to do with this present? If he tries to lift the pool, the juice will surely spill and cause a nasty stain. Besides, even if he could lift it without spilling anything, we've already made sure that the darn thing will not fit out the door or window unless it is turned on its side. Either this poor guy has to ladle the liquid, bit by bit, into smaller containers, or he simply has to drink an awful lot of grape juice.

We also know of excellent results obtained when this joke was done by placing the pool on the back seat of someone's Cadillac.

The Funny Bunnies

Naturally, we saved the best for last. Although it might prove difficult for you to attempt this gag in the grand style with which it was carried out at the famous Playboy Mansion in Chicago, there is a clever twist that will certainly allow everyone to work the gag at home. But first, the story as it developed in Bunny Land.

The Playboy Mansion in Chicago was infamous for its wild and unpredictable parties before the stakes were pulled up and moved to California. And newcomers to the risqué world of bouncing bunnies were usually subjected to an initiation of sorts that really amounted to nothing more than an elaborate practical joke. Once having passed the test at a Playboy party, the "victim" was, in effect, a member of the club and free to enjoy a good laugh when the next sucker came along. But make no mistake about it, these "victims" were not ordinary folk—rather the group included stage and screen stars, politicians and, as we shall see, one of the wealthiest men in America.

Especially for the gag, the Playboy masterminds built a unique room on the third floor of the Mansion. It had no windows or access points other than a narrow door and the walls and the ceiling were fully covered with mirrors. The other prime ingredient was an overly-voluptuous bunny who, in addition to her bunny talents, was amazingly good at

GOTCHA!

by Peter Funt & Mike Shatzkin

The Stonesong Press
a division of Grosset & Dunlap, Inc.
51 Madison Avenue
New York, N.Y. 10010

GOTCHA!